In You, Lord, I take refuge…
You are my rock and my
fortress; for Your name's sake
lead and guide me.
Psalm 31:2,4

The intent and
purpose of this volume is to
give you faith, hope and
inspiration. Hopefully it will help bring
peace and tranquility into your life. May
it be a reminder of God's love, guidance
and His many blessings.

Our publications help to support our work
for needy children in over 120 countries
around the world. Through our
programs, thousands of children are
fed, clothed, educated, sheltered
and given the opportunity to
live decent lives.

Salesian Missions wishes to extend special thanks and gratitude to o
generous poet friends and to the publishers who have given us permission to repri
material included in this book. Every effort has been made to give prop
acknowledgments. Any omissions or errors are deeply regretted, and the publisher, up
notification, will be pleased to make the necessary corrections in subsequent edition

Cover photo: Bass Harbor Lighthouse, Acadia National Park, Maine
©DigitalVision/PictureQuest

First Edition Printed in the U.S.A. by Concord Litho Group, Concord, NH 03301.

Lead Us Safely Home
from the Salesian Collection

Compiled and Edited
by Jennifer Grimaldi

Illustrated by
Robert VanSteinburg, Russell Bushée,
Paul Scully, Frank Massa, Helen M.L. Kunic,
Geraldine Aikman, Maureen McCarthy,
and Bob Pantelone

Contents

Blossoms

I watched the blossoms of the trees
In colorful array,
And swaying with a gentle breeze
They seemed to softly say...

"Each blossom that our God hath made
Does beautify the land,
And every lovely, pastel shade
Is painted by His hand."

I loved to watch them on that day,
But knew that suddenly –
At season's end they'd fade away,
But saddened I'd not be...

For blossoms shed – they come and go,
And others then appear.
New peace, new life, God does bestow
Each season of the year.

Edna Massimilla

Our days are like the
grass; like flowers of
the field we blossom.
Psalm 103:15

7

Valley of Flowers

Memories of the valley of flowers
Viewed from the grassy knoll
Never fail to move me
And bring pleasure to my soul.

I can still vision the beautiful flowers
Shimmering in sun's bright glow
And see the birds soaring over
The valley of flowers below.

I remember the field of clover
And the smell of it, fresh and fair.
Memories are planted deep in me
And my mind still wanders there.

There is no place more beautiful,
Where the trees are looming towers
That grow beside the rocky stream
In the valley of the flowers.

Shirley Hile Powell

River of Tears

There's a crystal river in Heaven
That catches each tear that's shed,
Then rushes past God's golden meadows
To His waterfall overhead.
This waterfall then forms a rainbow
Which covers our sky in a mist,
Then falls ever gently upon us…
A river of tears, Heaven-kissed.

Ruth E. McDaniel

Those who sow in tears will
reap with cries of joy.
Psalm 126:5

Walk My Garden

I've no olives in my garden,
Nor figs upon my trees,
But I offer sun and shadow,
Fragrant blossoms, gentle breeze.

And the heart can swell with gladness
And the mind can take its rest.
There's contentment in my garden
Where no man is put to test.

In this garden there's no weeping,
There's no sorrow, there's no pain.
Take my hand and I will lead You
Through a peaceful world again.

You have walked in many gardens –
In the desert, by the sea;
Come, accept my invitation…
Walk my garden, Lord, with me.

Ruth Malan Clingerman

*For a sun and shield is the Lord God,
bestowing all grace and glory. The
Lord withholds no good thing from
those who walk without reproach.*
Psalm 84:12

Miracles

I believe in miracles... I see them every day –
When barren trees don leaves once more,
When waves caress a sandy shore
And seasons slip away.

I believe in miracles... I hear them everywhere –
The murmur of the talking trees,
And bird song on the evening breeze,
A small child's bedtime prayers.

I believe in miracles... I smell their rare perfumes –
Apple blossoms, clover fields,
The heady scents a vineyard yields
On Autumn afternoons.

I believe in miracles… their flavors tantalize –
Sun-ripened fruit on tree or vine,
A farm-fresh egg, a vintage wine,
Warm-from-the-oven pies.

I believe in miracles… the touch of Summer rain –
And after rain the warmth of sun,
Contentment when the day is done
And I'm at home again.

I believe in miracles… the simple and the grand –
The strength God gives to face life's woes,
The blessings that He bestows
With such a caring hand.

Alice J. Christianson

*Therefore I tell you, all that you
ask for in prayer, believe that you
will receive it and it shall be yours.*
Mark 11:24

13

These Make a Home

The love of parents, dear and true,
To dwell beneath the skies of blue,
Country meadows, vast and wide,
The wonder of God's countryside,
Kindness, caring, childhood dreams,
The happiness of magic scenes...

Touch of beauty, hopes to keep,
Confidence, believing reaps,
Memories we cherish still,
Valleys deep, a climbing hill,
Yesterdays we treasured so,
Sun at dawning, nights aglow...

Family that's ever dear,
Happy moments ever near,
Laughter, sorrow – bits of each,
Pleasures close – some out of reach,
Togetherness – sometimes alone...
'Tis all of these that make a home.

Garnett Ann Schultz

*Happy the chosen ones You bring to dwell in Your
courts. May we be filled with the good things of
Your house, the blessings of Your holy temple!*
Psalm 65:5

The Blessings in a Smile

A smile, it can do many things,
This I found is true.
It can say, "I really care,"
To someone who is blue.

It can bond to perfect strangers
As they pass along the way.
It can tell a weary soul,
"I send God's love your way."

It can touch a broken, hurting heart,
And bring it hope renewed.
You have this "gift" upon your face…
Today, use it for God's good.

Mary Ann Jameson

Wings of Faith

I know a little secret
Of how to make faith grow –
Fold each hand and bend both knees
With your head bowed low.

Keep prayer in both heart and mind.
With God communicate.
Remember you must listen
And for an answer – wait!

Have God centered in your life,
Surrender to the King,
Yield your life to God on high…
Your faith will take to wing!

Carol Zileski

*For through the Spirit,
by faith, we await the
hope of righteousness.
Galatians 5:5*

17

My Little Country Home

It's often that I wander back
To visit for a while,
Back to my little country home
Where things were out of style.

There were no fancy linens
Or carpet on the floor,
No crystal chandelier that shined,
But we had love and more.

18

Our quilts were sewn by hand with care,
Each patch a lovely sight,
And kept us warm and comfortable
Upon a Winter night.

I still can see a lamplight glow,
A Bible by our bed,
I still recall its sacred trust
And scriptures Mother read.

Our home was just a humble house,
But we felt safe, secure,
And children all, both large and small,
Knew love and kindness pure.

Our home is still my castle and
My treasured memories,
And I can visit now and then –
My family waits for me.

Katherine Smith Matheney

Take Time

It only takes a moment
To make a day worthwhile,
To say a word in kindness,
To flash a friendly smile.

It only takes a moment
To watch a child at play,
To stop and smell the flowers
That bloom along your way.

It only takes a moment
To offer God a prayer,
To thank Him for His goodness,
To know you're in His care.

Beverly J. Anderson

As for me, when I came to you it was not
out of any favor on my part, but because
it was God's will. So continue to thank
Him every day; praise Him with song.
Tobit 12:18

20

Troubled Heart

When your heart is troubled
And no one seems to care,
Don't believe it for a moment,
For God is always there.

If trouble gets you down
And life does seem so bleak,
Lift your eyes to Heaven,
The face of God now seek.

In your soul you'll know Him
And peace will fill your heart,
If you believe in Him
And try to do your part.

He never will forsake you –
That's a promise He has made.
Lift your heart this very day,
Then watch your troubles fade.

Bernice Laux

Relieve the troubles of my heart;
bring me out of my distress.
Psalm 25:17

I Am Thankful for the Trees

The morning arose in a whisper of gold,
So tranquil and peacefully fair;
Mesmerized I watched its grandeur unfold,
Then I thankfully murmured a prayer.

From my window I watched the sun rising,
Easing slowly up out of the east,
And I saw a red-breasted robin
Alight on the feeder to feast.

The trees seemed to shimmer with foliage,
Greening and bathing in dew,
And my garden was bursting with blossoms
In colors of every hue.

How often we all take for granted
The treasures that only God made,
With never a thought to be thankful
For flowers and trees that give shade.

But if these were all taken from us,
What a colorless world it would be;
Therefore, from now on I will thank Him
For each flower, robin, and tree.

Ruth Gillis

It became beautiful and stately in its
spread of foliage, for its roots were
turned toward abundant water.
Ezekiel 31:7

Thank You, Lord

Thank You, Lord, for giving me
The courage to face each day,
The strength to carry me onward
And the vision to light my way.
My burdens are sometimes hard to bear,
But they may be a blessing by far,
For I've found a light inside of me
That burns like the brightest star.

Nancy Moran

My Daily Prayer

Oh Lord, grant me Thy infinite peace,
Let all my contentions and worries cease;
Fill me with Your love and grace,
And help me to conquer the woes I face.

Let not the sun on my anger set
So I will have no remorse or regret;
Let me live my life for You above
And for those whom I dearly love.

Let me be a light that shines
For You, oh Lord, and for all of mankind
And for those who really love me true,
Regardless of the things I do.

Help me to be thankful in heart and mind
For all of the beauty that I find.
Help me to live in goodness day to day,
For these things, dear Lord, I daily pray.

Shirley Hile Powell

*With his every deed he offered thanks to God Most
High, in words of praise. With his whole being he
loved his Maker and daily had His praises sung.*
Sirach 47:8

25

Sunsets

The constant crash of ocean waves,
A star-filled Autumn sky,
An eagle soaring through the air,
A sailboat drifting by…

The first snowfall of Winter,
A budding tree in Spring,
Raindrops on my window,
Birds that sweetly sing…

All these things I treasure,
Yet, I think the best
Of all God's rich creations
Are His glorious sunsets.

Mary Ann Jameson

Seize the Moment

Seize the moment when it comes,
It may never come again.
Do not waste it or cause regret
As you look back to "when."

Seize the moment, make it count,
Rescue some soul today.
Let lonely souls know of God's love
Whene'er they come your way.

Don't pass up opportunities
That God may bring to you,
For everything is planned by Him
And His every word is true.

He has a plan for you, my friend,
Each moment of your day,
So seize these moments, use them well
To give His love away.

Helen Gleason

*Conduct yourselves wisely
toward outsiders, making
the most of the opportunity.
Colossians 4:5*

Autumn's Falling Leaves

The Autumn leaves are falling now
In places far and near,
A carnival of colors bright
Our hearts will e'er hold dear.

I watch them whirl and twirl around
Like dancers at a ball
And wonder who will pick them up
When on the lawn they fall.

Small creatures come in playful moods
And scamper through the leaves
That children toss up in the air
From piles beneath the trees.

When evening comes, leaves heaped high,
We dine in campfire style;
Marshmallows toasted golden brown
Make all the work worthwhile.

Bright Autumn leaves are tumbling down,
So soon they disappear;
Mother Nature's way of telling us
Winter's drawing near.

Kay Hoffman

Shades of Autumn

Autumn colors, unsurpassed,
Always disappear too fast;
Trees in ever-changing hues
Capture Fall's resplendent views.

October's brilliant scenery
Is an Autumn guarantee;
Tapestries beyond compare
Show off Fall's fantastic flair.

The beauty of the season flies,
Vanishing before my eyes;
As Autumn shades intertwine
Around snow-white Winter shine.

Nora M. Bozeman

Thank the Lord

Thank the Lord for little favors
That He does for you each day
That are gifts of grace and blessings
To endear your life and way;
He is ever, always, mindful
Of our recklessness and greed,
And the weakness of our spirit
And His need to intercede.

Thank Him, and be always grateful
At the end of every day
For the love and care He showed you
At your labors and your play,
And be ever, ever grateful
For His love, so proven true,
That awakens you each morning
And abides in all you do.

Michael Dubina

A Seed That's Sown With Love

A seed that's sown with love will bear
The sweetest fruit, they say,
And produce a solid harvest
One golden Autumn day.

It's said the rose remembers
The dust from which it came,
And every ear of ripening corn
Knows its Master's name.

The farmer tills the earth, it's true,
And he may work the sod,
But no one owns the earth –
It is a gift of God!

From Eden to the present,
God's blessings have been seen
Each time the snows have melted
And earth again turns green.

Like the lilies of the field,
We're creations from above,
Mere stewards in God's paradise,
Sowing seeds with love.

Clay Harrison

Recipe for Living

A cup full of patience,
A portion of dreams,
A teaspoon of planning,
A few idle schemes,
A wee bit of thinking,
Some books of your own,
A serving of lectures,
A place to call home...
Some health is important,
A mixture of charms,
A spoon of persistence,
A heart soft and warm,
A faith in tomorrow,
A smile for today,
Believing and trusting
Each step of the way...
Some keen understanding,
A blue sky above,
A vision unequalled,
A heart full of love,
A serving of knowledge,
A questioning mind...
'Tis these that make up living,
All nicely combined.

Garnett Ann Schultz

*Your understanding covered the
whole earth, and, like the sea,
filled it with knowledge.*
Sirach 47:15

Shed a Little Light Upon the Path

Too many words are left unspoken.
Too many feelings seldom shared.
Too many hearts are left there, broken.
Too few told of God's great care.
Spread a little cheer today, my dear.
Shed a little light upon the path.
Cast a little joy about the earth –
Without unhappiness and wrath!
Share the gift of love God's given
That's bestowed on us from above!
Share the story of redemption –
And watch God's peace descending like a dove!

Verle Elizabeth Davis

Thank You

Thank You, dear Father,
For so many things –
For babies and sunlight
And butterfly wings,
For snowflakes and seashells,
For hummingbirds, too,
Hot cups of coffee
And skies, clear and blue,
For laughter and giggles,
For kisses, so sweet,
Choirs of children,
Warm food to eat,
For family and loved ones,
The hug of a friend...
Dear Father, this list
Could run without end.
Your blessings are many,
I've barely begun,
But, dear Father, God,
Thank You most for Your Son,
That He came and He lived
From His throne high above
To tell of Your caring,
Your patience, Your love.

Bea Lotz

We thank You, God, we give thanks;
we call upon Your name, declare
Your wonderful deeds.
Psalm 75:2

My "Pot of Gold"

Dear Lord, I come to thank Thee
For Your wonders from above,
The clear, blue sky, the green-leafed trees,
This wondrous land I love.

I see Your great creations
In lovely birds that sing,
And all the glories of this world,
And in every living thing.

The rainbow's hues as they appear
Against a sky of rain,
The pasteled clouds of pink and gold
Against the desert plains.

The mountains high, the still, cool glades,
The oceans as they roar…
These are the cherished things
That I am thankful for.

In Nature, You have worked
Creation to its best,
It lifts and feeds my spirit
And gives my very being rest.

But let me not forget
Thy most precious gift to me,
That "pot of gold" that is my soul,
That I offer up to Thee.

Phyllis Mellina

*You are my God, I give You thanks;
my God, I offer You praise.*
Psalm 118:28

Keep My Eyes on You

When my neighbor lets me down,
As he will sometimes do,
Give me patience with him
And keep my eyes on You.

When a Winter's day seems dreary
And the sun is hiding, too,
When I begin to grumble and complain,
Lord, keep my eyes on You.

For though this world holds heartaches,
Tears and sorrows, too,
I have the strength to persevere
When I keep my eyes on You.

Connie J. Kirby

The River

Flowing along between its banks,
Unhurried and trouble free,
The river follows its guided course
And makes its way to the sea.

Each of us flows in a river of time,
Unhurried or rushed and complaining.
Wanting to do more than we possibly can,
Ever stressful and straining.

Too soon we appear before God's throne
And find in our rush to live
We rushed past chances for kindness and help
And chances to love and forgive.

Let us relax in the love of God
And notice opportunity
To see the Lord in those that we meet
And treat Him tenderly.

Margaret Peterson

*May He rule from sea to
sea, from the river to the
ends of the earth.*
Psalm 72:8

Jesus Understands

My Savior knows my every need,
He notes the tears that fall;
He knows when sorrow overwhelms
And heeds my anguished call.

He cares when I am faint of heart
And hope is almost gone;
He understands my loneliness
As gray clouds hide the dawn.

'Tis then His nearness comforts me
In such a blessed way,
Assuring me He'll share my grief
And never from me stray.

Within the shelter of His arms
There's refuge from my fears,
As Jesus soothes my broken heart
And wipes away my tears.

His presence brings sweet peace to me,
His love becomes the light
That penetrates my troubled soul
And lifts the veil of night!

Beverly J. Anderson

*Those who trust in Him shall
understand truth, and the
faithful shall abide with Him
in love: Because grace and
mercy are with His holy ones,
and His care is with the elect.*
Wisdom 3:9

43

Heartfelt

Oh violin, how sweetly
You soothe the pining soul.
How sweet is your dear melody.
How much the strings must know.

How pretty are the birds that sing,
Their music fills the air.
Just one other gift that gives
A present to the ear.

How overwhelming are the blooms
That paint the hills and sides,
The vines that climb the purple cliffs
Where hues and scents collide.

'Tis then the heart is flowing,
'Tis then the soul is free,
'Tis then the air is giddy
With Nature's majesty.

James Joseph Huesgen

Finding the Silver Lining

Our Lord of mercy? Yes, He is!
And more, a God of grace;
For there we find that extra goodness,
Wherein are blessings laced.

We get forgiveness at His cross;
Mercy then wraps us 'round –
But His love still yearns to give,
And there His grace is found!

To know the depths of His dear love
Eludes the human mind,
For all our trials are mixed with grace
And in the end we find…

That even trials show forth His grace,
God-given for our refining,
For after they have worked our good –
We find their silver lining!

Lynn Fenimore Nuzzi

*When you hearken to the voice of the
Lord, your God, all these blessings will
come upon you and overwhelm you.*
Deuteronomy 28:2

The Flower of Love

Within the garden of my heart
I planted a little seed;
The packet read: THE FLOWER OF LOVE,
Of which each heart has need.

I sowed it very carefully,
Then breathed a little prayer
That it would grow till not a weed
Could find a mooring there.

Loise Pinkerton Fritz

My Dream House

My house of dreams stands midst the pines
'Neath azure-laden skies.
A path of love about it winds,
Comforting to weary minds.

My little door, a knocker bears
Upon the snow-white wood.
The golden sun outshines all cares
That would grow there if they could.

My little garden blooming
With roses of red hue,
All the plants a-growing
Are love's message from You.

My house of dreams stands midst the pines
'Neath the clear, starlit skies.
With evening's breath, I draw the blinds,
Keeping within love's lullabies.

Hazel K. Boyd

When cares increase within me,
Your comfort gives me joy.
Psalm 94:19

The Little Gifts of Cheer

I do not need a violin
To play a happy tune;
I only need a sunny day
To chase away my gloom.

The laughter of a little child,
A kitten dozing near,
Sweet birdsong in my apple tree
Can fill my heart with cheer.

A violet blooming on my sill,
Pink roses 'round my door,
A cup of tea shared with a friend –
What heart could wish for more?

Sometimes our gift of cheer is in
Something nice we do;
You cannot help someone without
It rubbing off on you.

Yet, often in our hurried pace
We cast these gifts away
Or trade them off for something new
To brighten up our day.

But I have come to know at last
What helps my heart to smile –
It's just the little gifts of cheer
That have the sweetest style.

Kay Hoffman

Look to Tomorrow

Each day you sit and ponder
The wrongs that you've been dealt
Is a day that you're subtracting
From the future owed yourself.

Each day you shun your neighbor
Deprives you of the chance
To form a lasting friendship
Or invite a pleasing glance.

Life's too short to dwell on
The hurts that filled the past,
But should be spent on building
Happy memories that can last.

You can find sweet comfort knowing
That you've done your very best
To make your life worth sharing,
And to God can leave the rest.

Catherine Janssen Irwin

Spring Blessings

Spring unfolds her blessings
When wintertime is o'er,
And days that hold her miracles
Are just outside my door.

Spring unfolds her beauty
Hanging blossoms on the trees;
Flower gardens begin to bloom
And perfume evenings' breeze.

Spring unfolds her magic
When songbirds start to sing,
For a multitude of blessings
God gives with His gift of Spring.

Nora M. Bozeman

Blessed be the God and Father of our Lord
Jesus Christ, who has blessed us in Christ
with every spiritual blessing in the heavens.
Ephesians 1:3

In Your House

I love it in Your house, Lord,
Where I can be with You.
I know that You are with me,
No matter what I do.

And being here is special;
I feel Your presence here,
And I'm among Your people,
So beautiful and dear.

I come here to meet with You
And hear Your word so true.
Your spirit fills my heart
As I draw near to You.

You give me strength to endure
All that faces me each day.
I know that You are with me
And guide me on my way.

Thank You, Heavenly Father,
For the constant love You give.
I'll give You all the glory
Every day that I shall live.

Dona M. Maroney

For the spirit of the Lord fills the
world, is all-embracing, and
knows what man says.
Wisdom 1:7

If

If God can make a rainbow
And create a sky so blue,
Made in His own image,
There are things that we can do.

If God can make a rosebud
With fragrance sweet and rare,
We can spread joy and happiness
Here and everywhere.

If God can make a sturdy oak
To withstand any storm,
Then we can smile and overcome
When with grief we're torn.

If God could sacrifice His Son
To teach us how to love,
Then we can face most anything
With His strength from above.

Ruth Moyer Gilmour

He gives safety and support.
He sustains the mighty by
His strength, and His eyes
are on their ways.
Job 24:23

My Thank-You Prayer

When I lay down at night
Wondering what to pray,
I try to thank the Lord above
For whatever happened that day.
It could be a simple thing,
A bud upon a flower
Or perhaps some time to think,
A peaceful, quiet hour.
It might be that our humble home,
Small though it may be,
Was filled with joy and laughter
For everyone to see.
If it was unpleasant,
I thank Him anyway
For all the lessons learned
On that fateful day.
And when I'm done that night
With my thank-you prayer,
My heart is filled to overflowing
With all the love He shared.

Rebecca Sweeney

*I thank You for You answered me;
You have been my Savior.
Psalm 118:21*

55

September's Door Is Open

September's door is open,
It bids us enter in.
To Summer's month of August,
It is the next of kin.

Upon its floor, dew-tinted,
We view the harvest yield;
Apples, pumpkins, sweet corn
Upon September's fields.

September's door is open;
In hope and prayer we kneel
That we might know the blessings
Of this, His bountiful yield.

Loise Pinkerton Fritz

I Thank You, God

I thank You, God, for life and health
And love I have today,
For this great land of freedom,
And the privilege to pray.

I thank You for my home
And for my daily bread.
I thank You for the Bible,
From which my soul is fed.

I thank You for the gift of life
Through Jesus Christ, Your Son.
The loving sacrifice He made
Was made for everyone.

Help me accept the gifts You gave,
May my voice Your praises sing,
And may I with true thanksgiving
Seek Your will in everything.

Frances Culp Wolfe

*Sing praise to the Lord,
you faithful; give thanks
to God's holy name.*
Psalm 30:5

Summer Days Beside the Sea

I strolled along the sandy beach
And breathed the salty air;
I watched the children as they shaped
Sand castles everywhere!

O'erhead, the sea gulls dipped and soared
'Cross skies of azure blue,
While in the distance I could see
A lonely sailboat, too.

I watched the tide roll in and out,
Bringing seashells by the score;
I stooped to gather them
And watched as lofty kites did soar.

It was a dreamy, carefree day
With troubles put to rest;
Those lazy days beside the sea
Most surely were the best!

I delight in fragrant flowers of Spring,
Fall and Winter scenes of yore,
But I enjoy the Summer days
Beside the sea much more.

Mary S. Chevalier

Giving

"Give, Said the Little Stream…"
We sang long, long ago;
So little did I realize
The seeds this song had sown.
Seeds sown deep within my heart,
Concerning joys of giving;
Seeds that sprouted into bloom
And made my life worth living.

"Give, Said the Little Stream…"
I hear it echo still.
Though small, it made fields greener still
While hurrying down the hill.
Singing, singing on its way,
It kept on giving, giving;
May we, just like this little stream,
Make giving part of living.

Loise Pinkerton Fritz

Shepherd, Lead Us

We can go through life each day,
Deciding whom to trust…
Or we can lift our hearts to God
And let Him choose for us.

It's a matter of perception
And knowing how to pray…
God will never let us down
Or lead His sheep astray.

The road that's set before us
Is sometimes less than straight…
But God will guide us every day;
He knows which path to take.

A sheep can trust the Shepherd
To lead His flock to grace…
Trusting Him is all we need;
He's with us in this place.

Jill Lemming

I will appoint over you shepherds after
My own heart, who will shepherd you
wisely and prudently.
Jeremiah 3:15

The Power of Prayer

Gentle Savior, loving Lord,
Have mercy on Your child!
The waves are crashing overhead –
The wind is blowing wild.
I cannot see the light of day,
For darkness fell so fast;
No one can hear my cries for help
Above the stormy blast.

I'm reaching out to You, O God;
You are my only hope!
I can't hold out much longer,
And alone, I cannot cope.
Oh, send some sign that You are here
So I will not despair –
Give me reason to hold on…
And know You truly care.

But wait, what's that I see in this dark night
That wasn't there before?
It looks to be a beacon bright,
Beckoning me to shore!

My fervent prayer was heard! Praise God!
My strength has been renewed.
I've seen the power of prayer,
And I know what I must do...
Follow the light back to the shore,
Never stray from its beam!
It is my one and only refuge,
And I see within its gleam...

A reflection on the billows
That tells me all's not lost,
For I see glowing upon the waves...
The outline of a cross.

Denise A. DeWald

*The effectual fervent
prayer of a righteous
man availeth much.*
James 5:16

Home

A house can be a mansion
With a crystal chandelier,
But a home can be a cottage
With windows shining clear!

A house can be three stories
With a wide and curving stair,
But a home is warm and cozy,
With a worn-in easy chair!

It isn't space that makes a home,
Or elegant decor,
But love and trust that live within
And greet you at the door!

Ina Murray

Each Day Is a Gift

I read this morning, "Each day is a gift;"
We should open it with prayer.
It may be the day which offers us hope;
To some, it will bring despair.

We know that life is not all roses;
The bush has many a thorn,
And each day will be full of surprises
From the moment we are born.

Today is the one we must live to the full
And not seek our own selfish desire.
Give the "Bread of Life" with every deed you do;
Warm the cold-hearted by your fire.

When the sun goes down and night grows dark,
Kneel again by your bed to pray.
If you failed in something, God always forgives,
And tomorrow will be a new day.

Elaine Fowser

*Give us each day our
daily bread.
Luke 11:3*

Beholden to the Golden Leaves

Bright, golden leaves are all I need
To start my Autumn days;
Along the paths they lie in state
In season's grand displays,
But soon they're joined by reds and browns,
First scattered by faint breeze,
Then swirled by winds of hazy dawns
Which rustle through the trees.
November hints of dusty cool
As leaves blend lifelessly,
Mosaic of a hued demise
Which greets eternity.
December bids when come the snows
To blanket all scenes white;
I watch with sadness as the leaves
Are taken from my sight.

Henry W. Gurley

Indian Summer

Season of splendor that makes my heart sing
For the beauty the Indian Summer does bring,
Crimson and amber and gold leaves fall,
Of birds that chatter and winds that call.
It thrills me through with such delight,
Magic colors on an Autumn night,
Rustling leaves like lullabies
Respond to the warmth of Autumn skies.
Imbued with colors as Nature conceives
Messages of joy my heart receives.
The harvest moon reflects once more
The bountiful wealth of Autumn's store!
And sleeping blooms of Summer lie
And whisper to Autumn a faint good-bye.
The longing and zest of this season at last
Lingers awhile, then fades in the past.
Treasures of earth you will only find
In the Indian Summer that God designed!

Gene Appleby

*I will delight and rejoice in
You; I will sing hymns to
Your name, Most High.*
Psalm 9:3

First Give Thanks

To worry and fret
Is hardly the way
To tell God my needs
While I'm trying to pray.

When life gets real hard
And seems rather grim,
I know that it's best
If I focus on Him.

When I first give thanks,
My spirit will rise,
Then all of my problems
Seem smaller in size.

I shan't take for granted
The new morning light,
Nor the clouds, nor the wind,
Nor the eagle in flight.

With full appreciation,
I'll sing a new song,
As my hope and my faith
Will grow to be strong.

I will give thanks
Before I receive,
For I know that God
Is caring for me.

Joyce Mary Ecochard

Pack Your Smile

Be prepared for the journey of life,
Mile after mile after mile.
Though the journey contains good and bad,
Remember to pack your smile.

Whether you're sailing on the deep, blue sea
Or sitting alone in the dark,
The Spirit can give you a smile for your face
And joy in the depths of your heart.

No matter what comes, no matter what goes,
Remember God's there all the while.
He loves you so and He's in control,
So remember to pack your smile.

Idella Pearl Edwards

Autumn Requests

Dear Lord, my needs are very small…
So may I cite a few?
Give me a balmy Autumn day
And sky of cloudless blue.

Oh, let me feel the gentle rain
Fall softly on my face,
And sprinkle gold dust through the trees
And every hidden place.

Just let me see the wild geese fly
With rhythmic wings in flight;
I want to hear the crickets chirp
When day succumbs to night.

This is the season I love best…
When trees are all aflame,
Then Nature paints her masterpiece
To glorify Your name!

Gene Appleby

*I will praise You with all my
heart, glorify Your name
forever, Lord my God.*
Psalm 86:12

A State of Mind

Age is truly a state of mind,
A conscious attitude.
It's a matter of perception
That determines our mood.

Some see the glass half empty
And quickly they complain,
But others see the glass half full
And sing a sweet refrain.

Some are content to live in the past
And they learn nothing new,
While others give thanks for each new day
And do what they can do.

Some say, "I can't!" and never try
While others say, "Why not?"
The wise ones reap the blessings
That faith and prayer have wrought.

Youth cannot be recaptured
Once the years depart,
But it truly is our state of mind
That keeps us young at heart!

Clay Harrison

Sweet Assurance

Life is like a storybook;
Each day a page unfolds.
We never know beforehand
What scenarios it holds.
But whatever be the drama,
Filled with bounty or with tares,
There's comfort and assurance
That our Father always cares.

Virginia Borman Grimmer

Winds of Fate

Burdens are scattered like fallen leaves
And are lifted by the winds of fate.
Relief is sent from our loving God
Which comes never too soon nor too late.

If we but put our trust in Him
And dwell on the love He gave,
Like the winds of fate, He will lift us up,
While our souls He will surely save.

One never knows what tomorrow brings
But if God has us in His care,
We'll be filled with an unsurpassed love,
Like a jewel that is exquisite and rare.

So dwell not on tomorrow, friends,
But concentrate on today.
Live life according to God's plans
And follow in His loving ways.

Shirley M. Powell

*I trust in Your faithfulness. Grant
my heart joy in Your help, that I
may sing of the Lord, "How good
our God has been to me!"*
Psalm 13:6

My Wings

Lord, You put flight
Into my wings.
You are the reason
My heart sings.

You fill the longings
In my soul.
You bring the joy
That makes me whole.

You're all I need
My whole life through;
You give the strength
For all I do.

Each day to me,
New life You bring.
You are the wind
Beneath my wings.

Helen Gleason

Be at Peace

Oh, worrisome spirit, be at peace,
For God is taking care of you.
He sees each trial and burden
And knows exactly what to do.

Release each problem to Him,
As you bow your head to pray,
Then, with assurance of His goodness,
March on to greet the day!

He sends angels to attend to you
When the way seems dark and drear,
And if the fires of pain assail,
Be at peace, God is near!

There's not a problem He can't handle,
So unlike you and me.
Oh, troubled soul, be at peace –
Reach out to Him and you will see!

Linda C. Grazulis

The God of peace be with
all of you. Amen.
Romans 15:33

On Wings of Night

The stars appear on wings of night,
A golden moon is shining bright,
As little creatures of the day
Are still as twilight finds its way.
The birds at rest within the trees,
We marvel at the gentle breeze.

On wings of night, the shadows fall,
A dark descending over all,
A time of peace and quiet still,
A magic glow atop the hill.
It seems a gentle, fragile time,
A miracle that's yours and mine.

God ever smiles from there above,
'Tis then we know His wondrous love.
The busy day is cast aside,
A fairer beauty shall abide,
As darkness takes the place of light
And blessings come on wings of night.

Garnett Ann Schultz

*Yours the day and Yours
the night; You set the moon
and sun in place.*
Psalm 74:16

When Skies Are Gray
and Snowflakes Fall

Oh, how I miss the hummers now
That Winter's come to stay.
I hate to take their feeders down
And pack them all away.

My acrobatic feathered friends
Go south this time of year,
And as I watch them fly away
I wipe away a tear.

When skies are gray and snowflakes fall
Upon the barren trees,
My thoughts return to warmer days
With hummers on the breeze.

I know one day in sunny May
How happy I will be,
For my ruby-throated friends
Once more will visit me.

Clay Harrison

Winter Comes Calling

Winter knocked upon my door,
Bringing cold and snow galore.
She looked just like an Eskimo
In her hat of frosted snow.

She wore a cloak of ermine white
And silver-dusted trees at night.
She sparkled every field and stream
With diamonds from a bright moonbeam.

A masterpiece of art was she
Bedecked in snow-white finery.
She displayed her silent charms
Then fell asleep in springtime's arms.

Nora M. Bozeman

From the North the splendor
comes, surrounding God's
awesome majesty!
Job 37:22

My House Is Just a Little House

My house is just a little house,
But God knows where I live.
Such blessings He bestows on me;
Abundantly He gives.
And oh, I love my little house!
It is so cozy-warm,
With God's angels watching o'er it
To keep me safe from harm.
I do praise God, yes, each mealtime
Because my table's spread;
I give to Him my gratitude
For gifts of daily bread.
The clock ticks away the hours,
I hear the cricket's song,
My heart is oh, so happy –
I praise God all day long.

Now I shall put the kettle on
And make a pot of tea;
I'll go and ask some neighbors in
To share it all with me.
I take joy in the little things
That come with each new day –
The sunshine, bird songs and rainbows –
And so I kneel to pray.
Such blessings He bestows on me;
Abundantly He gives.
My house is just a little house,
But God knows where I live.

Mary E. Herrington

*As for me and my
household, we will
serve the Lord.*
Joshua 24:15

Gift

For God so loved
The world, He gave
His only Son,
Our souls to save.
Pause now, dear ones.
Let us reflect
Upon the Christ;
Pay Him respect.

Quiet ourselves
To quell the din
Of daily stress;
Invite Him in.
Open the chambers
Of our heart,
Receive the love
He will impart.

Yes, there are problems
And unrest,
So many trials
To try and test
That challenge
The faith we know,
Threatening love
We want to show.

Pause and accept
His Gift.... Release
Ourselves to know
His inner peace.
For God so loved
He gave His Son
To give His peace
And joy, dear one!

Anna Lee Edwards McAlpin

Quiet Mornings

In the early morning hours
When birds are singing sweet
And train whistles fill the hushness
Of this quiet dark and deep...

I think of all my blessings;
Each heartbeat is a gift.
A new day now is dawning.
My life, so full of bliss.

Oh Lord, I am so grateful
You've let me live today.
I know there's much for me to do,
As I travel on life's way.

May I always serve You, Lord,
No matter what the task.
You want me to be faithful,
For that is all You ask.

Mary Ann Jameson

O Lord, have pity on us, for
You we wait. Be our strength
every morning, our salvation
in time of trouble!
Isaiah 33:2

Sweet, Fragrant Spring

Sweet, fragrant Spring has come again,
Our Winter-weary hearts to win.
She flaunts her beauty, anxious to please,
Flings lilac perfume on April's breeze.

An artist with a special flare,
She fashions flowers wondrous fair,
Calls honeybees to come and sup
Sweet nectar from each dainty cup.

Butterflies, flowers, honeybees,
Robins singing in the trees;
Scenes of beauty we like to see
She sends "with love" to you and me.

I'm told her home's that golden shore,
That she will live forevermore,
But visit here for just a while
To bring each face a happy smile.

And we in awesome wonder see
How quick she makes the Winter flee,
For who can hold to thoughts of gray
When sweet, young Spring has come our way?

Kay Hoffman

A Breath of Spring

April bathes in the breath of Spring
And borrows a robin's song to sing.
She lilac-lines the lanes with care
And scatters tulips everywhere.

April emeralds fields and hills
And golds the garden with daffodils.
She wears a glistening dewdrop gown
With white-washed daisies for her crown.

April bathes in the breath of Spring,
Awakens every living thing;
Then fancy-free, she wends her way
Into the merry month of May.

Nora M. Bozeman

His Love Will Light the Way

His love will light the way
As we travel through this life.
His love will guide our path
Through days filled with toil and strife.
As we struggle through the valleys
Where our fears shut out the light,
His love will light the way
And will make our pathway bright.

His love will light the way
As the billows 'round us roll,
As the storms of life are raging
And we feel out of control.
When we put our faith in Him
And in His strength alone,
His love will light the way
And will lead us safely home.

Shirley W. Langley

God is light and in Him
is no darkness at all.
1 John 1:5

Beauty

Beauty surrounds us,
If we take the time to look.
We can see it in the valleys
And in every rippling brook.

We can see it in graceful birds
Soaring high in a cloudless sky.
A frisky, brown squirrel
Racing to a leafy tree nearby.

We can see it in flower buds
Hiding their glorious array,
Waiting for the perfect moment
Their beauty to display.

We can see it in little children
Laughing happily with glee,
Peacefully napping or
Sitting on Granddad's knee.

Yes, beauty surrounds us,
As God meant it to be,
If we will pause and look
And take the time to see.

Barbara Dickerson

*Charm and beauty delight
the eye, but better than either,
the flowers of the field.*
Sirach 40:22

I Hear Thee Knocking

I hear Thee knocking at my door;
I need Thee, precious Lord.
I ask Thee, Master, to come in,
For Thou art e'er adored.

I hear Thee knocking at my door;
I know that Thou art there.
My life I place in Thy sweet hand;
Come listen to my prayer.

I hear Thee knocking at my door,
Dear Savior, Lord divine.
Please enter in and heal me, Lord,
And make me ever Thine.

Hope C. Oberhelman

My Every Day

The best part of my every day
Is when I'm going home.
I count the footsteps all the way
From places where I've roamed.

The evening sunset settles low
And takes my cares away;
Then I thank God for all He's done
To bless my every day.

I'm thankful to our God above
For the wondrous gifts He's given.
My every day's filled with His love
That makes my life worth livin'.

Gertrude Blau Byram

Wear a Smile

Wear a smile of happiness
As through this life you go.
It doesn't cost a penny,
Yet sets your heart aglow,
Will quickly chase the clouds of gloom,
Put rainbows in your sky,
It's filled with special goodness
And ever lights your eye.

Wear a smile at dawning,
Beginning each new day,
Creating paths of sunshine
Along each weary way.
And then as twilight beckons
With starshine from above,
Find the evening quiet,
Rich in hope and love.

Hear the happy laughter
Of children at their play,
Take their hands and guide them,
Help them find the way.
Bits of joy and sunshine
Make your life worthwhile.
You'll be rich in blessings
If you wear a smile.

Garnett Ann Schultz

No treasure greater than a
healthy body; no happiness,
than a joyful heart!
Sirach 30:16

Never Doubt

Dear anxious one, head bowed in prayer,
Know that God is listening there.
He heeds the slightest prayer we pray;
It matters not if night or day.

He promises He'll meet our need,
But we must trust in Him to lead;
His path may not be one you'd choose;
Your hand in His, you cannot lose.

God loves you and He'll see you through;
He gave His Son to die for you.
Oh weary one, heart burdened with care,
Never doubt the power of prayer.

Kay Hoffman

God Is There

Hours turn into days,
Days turn into years.
Many roads we travel on,
Some with doubts and fears.
Though problems overwhelm us
And tensions fill our day,
There is someone to turn to,
Who will guide us on our way.

He's there in time of trouble,
He's there in deep duress.
You will find that God is near
And is always there to bless.

He's our light in the darkness,
A lamp unto our feet —
Our Lord is always there
To make our day complete.

Dorothy C. Deitz

*Your word is a lamp for my
feet, a light for my path.*
Psalm 119:105

His Gifts of Love

I will talk to all who will listen
To what I have to say,
In hopes my words will reach each heart
To guide and show the way.

I'll speak of His amazing grace,
Of His mercy and His love,
To let them know He's always there
As He watches from above.

He hears the prayer of this sinner
Who asks, with contrite heart,
To be freed of my transgressions,
And to make a brand-new start.

Soon the angel choirs will sing,
The trumpets will loudly sound,
For Jesus' love now fills my needs,
And new purpose I have found.

I'll now proclaim His mighty power,
Hear the Alleluias ring!
Then lift my hands to offer up
All the gifts His love will bring.

Angie Monnens

Answer when I call, my saving God.
In my troubles, You cleared a way;
show me favor, hear my prayer.
Psalm 4:2

Greater Than All Riches

What I have is precious,
A gift from God above,
A blessing sent from Heaven,
Wrapped tightly in God's love.

My family, they're safe harbor
From the storms that blow my way.
They comfort and they guide me,
And always for me pray.

My friends, my boon companions,
Who help me dry my tears,
Who share with me the love of God,
And help me persevere.

What blessed gifts from Heaven
Are my friends and family.
With grateful heart to You, dear Lord,
I give my thanks to Thee.

Mary Ann Jameson

Treasures Along the Seashore

Have you ever taken the time to notice
So many treasures along the shore –
Seashells which echo the rushing waves,
A gentle breeze and so much more?
The smell of the salty water
And sounds of the billowing tides,
The fog and misty ocean spray –
A seagull soaring nearby…
Walking barefoot on the sand –
Oops! A starfish slithers ashore.
Oft I wonder what other fascinating creatures
Lie upon the ocean's rocky floor.
All these tiny miracles –
God created each and every one
To teach us of His goodness
And to reveal His mighty love.

Linda C. Grazulis

The Miles and Years

I look back o'er the miles and years
And see where I have been.
I see again the smiles and tears
As I think back to "then."

So often on the path I chose
My life was surely blessed,
But it was when God led the way
I did my very best.

For He can see the miles ahead
That bruise our weary feet;
He sees beyond our vision
All the obstacles we meet.

I look back o'er the miles and years,
But they are gone forever.
The lessons that I learned somehow
Are all that time can't sever.

I know I serve a changeless God,
So on my knees I pray,
If I am blessed with miles and years,
Please guide me all the way.

Gertrude B. McClain

*You restore my strength. You
guide me along the right path for
the sake of Your name.*
Psalm 23:3

Hearing Soft Wind

God sprinkles dewdrops on the grass
And polishes lakes clear as glass.
He spreads cool shade beneath the tree
As resting places for you and me.

He shapes our minds to enjoy such things,
Like hearing a soft wind as it sings.
He plants love-thoughts in our hearts
So that all our selfishness departs.

God closes the days with star-filled nights;
He hangs up the moon to serve us light.
He touches our pain and it slips away –
Always, He hears us when we pray.

Rosa Nelle Anderson

Water Skaters and Dragonflies

I watched the little skaters
Skating on the pond;
The little water skaters,
Frolicking, every one.
They'd skim across the water,
Then sometimes they'd glide.
On this midsummer noontide,
It was a thrilling sight.

Two dragonflies approached me,
Then circled 'round and 'round;
Their black reticulated wings
Ne'er seemed to make a sound.
O'er the pond my cares soon skimmed
Just like the water skaters;
Then like dragonflies in flight,
I "winged" home to my labor.

I basked in sweet serenity,
These moments at this spot,
Marveling at the wondrous sights
Created by our God.

Loise Pinkerton Fritz

*Sing unto Him, sing psalms
unto Him, talk ye of all His
wondrous works.*
1 Chronicles 16:9

Love Is All That Matters

Born in a poor, forsaken place,
I slept on the hardwood floor.
The windows held no shining pane
And the cold came through the door.

My shoes were worn, my coat was thin,
My dress was ragged cotton,
My hair grew wild below my waist,
In a time almost forgotten.

A time our only wealth was love,
And family life, a treasure.
We fought to help each other live;
To give, our greatest pleasure.

A time now gone with passing days
That died for prosperous years,
And saw us go our separate ways,
Down a flowered path of tears.

If God should ask my heart's desire,
There's no blessing I'd love more
Than going home for one last night
To sleep on the hardwood floor!

Kate Watkins Furman

Falling Leaves

Down come the leaves, bright yellow and red,
Settling soon in a snug Winter bed,
Floating upon the wings of the breeze,
Twisting and turning with delicate ease.

I sit by my window, entranced by the sight,
And follow the course of beauty in flight,
To unite in array on grass that's still green –
No artist could paint a more beautiful scene.

Lester E. Bartholomew

On Wings of Faith

Dare to dream bright, lofty dreams
With purposeful intent;
Dare to plan a noble course
To take and to augment.

Dare to strive to be your best
In everything you do,
To value truth and honesty
So they'll reflect on you.

Dare to soar to greater heights
On wings of faith and love,
Knowing that God's guiding light
Is shining from above.

Vi B. Chevalier

*They that hope in the Lord will renew their
strength, they will soar as with eagles'
wings; they will run and not grow weary,
walk and not grow faint.*
Isaiah 40:31

Laughter Through the Tears

Friendship is a golden thread
That binds our hearts with love,
A bond that reaches to the stars
That twinkle high above.

Friends see the pain behind the smile
And come before we call
To walk with us that "extra mile"
And lift us when we fall.

Friends see beyond our failures
The person we can be,
And they never are too busy
To share a cup of tea.

Friends are the glue God gives us
To mend a broken heart,
The anodyne that sustains us
When our world falls apart.

Friendship is a precious thing
That lives beyond the years,
A looking glass that lets us see
The laughter through the tears.

Clay Harrison

God's Autumn Radiance

In joy I watch the woodland leaves
Adrift in jeweled jamborees;
Parading banners twist and fly
Into the shimmering morning-glory sky.

Rich colors whirl from treetops bare,
Their beauty burning windswept air.
In Autumn breeze, leaves tumble down –
Vermillion, bronze and chestnut brown.

Scarlet apple trees with fruit bend down,
Glowing pear trees flaunt each golden crown,
Bright, bittersweet blooms with heads held high,
As milkweed parachutes float by.

Dazzling maples in splendor along the lane
Wear frost-silvered halos once again.
Night echoes the whippoorwill's farewell call…
God's heavenly radiance spreads over all.

Elisabeth Weaver Winstead

Autumn Reflection

The winds of Autumn softly blow.
They whisper, "Soon there will be snow."

The sun sets early, nights are long.
The morning birds have ceased their songs.

The trees ablaze with Autumn gold,
But, soon it will be turning cold.

This time of year, it's time to pause,
And count the blessings that are ours...

For all the bounty that we see,
Good harvest, and for family.

These blessings come from God above,
And through all these, He shows His love.

Mary Ann Jameson

Show us, Lord, Your love;
grant us Your salvation.
Psalm 85:8

My Grand Cathedral

I have a grand cathedral
For myself and God alone;
It has no stained-glass windows,
No gold, nor polished stone.
No incense sweet, nor candles,
No carpet for my knees,
Just fragrant grass beneath my feet
And the beauty of tall trees.
Eloquently this quiet world
Tells of the Father's love.
In silence, all the stars speak out
From the darkened sky above.

Then gracefully they fade away,
Replaced with rosy light,
As emanating sunbeams
Whisk away the night.
How lovely is my Father's world
When morning breaks the skies,
And from my grand cathedral,
My morning prayers arise.

Gael Phaneuf

*Do you know? Have you heard?
The Lord is the everlasting God, the
Creator of the ends of the earth.*
Isaiah 40:28

Compassionate People

Compassionate people,
Warm-hearted and true,
Who enrich lives of others
With nice things they do.
Compassionate people,
So precious but few,
Who know in a crisis
The right thing to do.
Compassionate people
Who find joy in giving
And put others first
In their process of living.
When I count my life's blessings
From beginning to end,
I thank God for you,
My compassionate friend.

Ruth Moloney Cowgill

Our Thanks, Dear Lord

Dear Lord, we give our thanks to Thee
And praise You with good cheer,
For such a bountiful harvest
You have blessed us with this year.

We have so much to be thankful for
That mere words can only say
How I feel within my heart
On this Thanksgiving Day.

Thank You for our friends, dear Lord,
That mean so very much;
Bless our loving family
And keep them in Your touch.

Dear Lord, we give our thanks to Thee
And praise You as we should,
Thank You for Your blessings,
For the bad things and the good.

Help us serve and follow You
As we go along our way.
Bless all those present, Lord,
On this Thanksgiving Day.

Nell Ford-Hann

One of God's Best Secrets

The clouds like mighty trumpets
Blew in the Winter's first snow
And created an enchanting wonderland,
Making an architectural show.

The air was of purest white
That danced around in swirls
And made the ghostly-barren fields
A sea of giant, white furrows.

All of the thickened woodlands,
Once barren, naked, and brown,
Now glisten and sparkle with splendor
As the snowflakes drift around.

"Oh, let it snow!" cry the little ones.
It's a sight to see and feel.
It's one of God's best-kept secrets
That in the Winter He reveals.

Shirley Hile Powell

*Adorn yourself with grandeur
and majesty, and array yourself
with glory and splendor.*
Job 40:10

The Three Visitors

They came one lonely Winter's eve
When I was at wit's end;
They came because I was alone,
In need of a good friend.
The first came dressed in glory
With a cast of holy light.
She met me as I knelt in prayer –
Faith met me there that night.

I uttered such a broken prayer
I knew it wasn't good,
But then a feeling swept through me,
I felt I understood.

The words were not important,
Just what was in my heart.
Hope became my friend that night –
I knew we'd never part.

Love was my third companion;
She filled me so inside.
She gave me back my self esteem,
Filled me with Godly pride.
The three now travel with me,
Helping me along life's way.
They are the gifts my Father gives
As I turn to Him each day.

Nancy Watson Dodrill

Gentle Lord and Savior

When the world seems set against us
And no matter what we do,
Nobody seems to understand
What we are going through…
When plans that seemed so perfect
Do not materialize,
And dust of all our worn-out hopes
Keeps getting in our eyes…

It's time to re-evaluate
The way which we have come,
And start to count our blessings,
Which are greater far than some.
To hand our burden over
To the One whom we can trust,
And our gentle Lord and Savior
Will carry it for us.

Grace E. Easley

And God Created Them All

The wonders of Nature are mighty,
The soul of man they enthrall.
The mountains, the trees, the waters…
And God created them all.

The wonders of Nature are holy,
To the spirit they call.
The wind, the stars, a rainbow…
And God created them all.

Give thanks for the wonders of Nature,
For miracles large and small.
The earth abounds with treasures…
And God created them all!

Eleanor Torchia

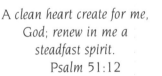

*A clean heart create for me,
God; renew in me a
steadfast spirit.*
Psalm 51:12

Healing Grace

How gentle is that healing grace
That comes from "God knows where,"
When all the remedies of earth
Have failed to ease despair.
It is a miracle of love,
An act of sacred heart,
That touches us with healing grace
No human can impart.

We rise from off a bed of pain
With smiles – instead of tears –
And walk again without restraints
Or crippling aches and fears.
And no one can explain this cure
That comes from "God knows where" –
It's just a healing grace of love
That heals us in its care.

Yet there are those who will proclaim,
"It's just a cure of time,"
While Christian hearts declare such cures
As healing grace, divine.
The lame are seen to rise and walk
From only faith and prayer
And miracles are made to be
From only "God knows where."

Michael Dubina

Heal me, Lord, that I may be
healed; save me, that I may be
saved, for it is You whom I praise.
Jeremiah 17:14

The Little Country Store

The oak trees grew around it,
Casting shapes of dappled shade,
And behind it ran a little brook
In which we used to wade.
Built of frame and shingles,
It was a humble store,
But it stocked all we needed,
And perhaps a little more.

It had a porch with railings
And kegs to sit upon,
A lazy, twirling ceiling fan,
A quaint, old-fashioned phone.
The glass jars on the counter
Gave one a tempting view
Of brightly colored candies
And ginger cookies, too.

The old icebox had plenty
Of orange soda pop.
There were balls and jacks for children
And kites and shiny tops.
The walls were lined with bolts of cloth
And matching spools of thread.
There were barrels of red apples
And the smell of homemade bread.

Folks had a way of visiting
Beneath its friendly roof.
You could learn who just got married
And which baby had a tooth.
And if it was companionship
That you were longing for,
It was never out of season
At the little country store.

Grace E. Easley

*Moreover, you are to provide
yourself with all the food that is
to be eaten, and store it away,
that it may serve as provisions
for you and for them.*
Genesis 6:21

A Full Day With God

Fill my days with sunshine bright,
With flowers in wondrous array –
Each in its own colorful hue
And all in a fragrant bouquet!
Fill my nights with moonlit skies,
With stars and the Milky Way –
With a peaceful sleep and rested mind
To help me greet the new day.
Fill my hours within each day
With joy and praise to Thee
For each and every blessing sent
From You, dear Lord, to me.
And may I use each minute, each second,
Throughout the entire day
To share Thy love and peace with those
I meet along the way!

Mary Chevalier

*Guide me in Your truth and teach
me, for You are God my Savior. For
You I wait all the long day, because
of Your goodness, Lord.*
Psalm 25:5

128